My Heart At Ease

Jeffrey McAndrew

Dedication

This book of poems is dedicated to my mother, Jane Elizabeth McAndrew. She was the first hand I held, her body my home before I took my first breath. She is an infinite well of caring and love in my life. Her sense of humor, positive outlook on life and love of great poetry will stay with me always. Mom, I would be nowhere without your patient love and caring guidance.

Foreword

Quite a few years ago, I met Jeffrey McAndrew when my co-host and I interviewed him for our YouTube interview show called "Author Showcase." I quickly realized I had read his book <u>Our Brown-Eyed Boy</u> when I was looking for books about children with autism. As we are both local authors, we kept in touch. I kept tabs on him as he published a couple more books. Still I was surprised that he had taken on this project of writing 100 poems in a year. I had only known of his nonfiction and his fiction work. Should I have been surprised? Of course not. Jeffrey is a singer/songwriter.

That is evident in that many of his poems are lyrical. I can almost hear a guitar accompanying his hymn-like stanzas.

Jeffrey's poems in this collection are upbeat and encouraging as they deal with today's problems. Even the poems that turn inward and celebrate his life and his loved ones seem to be a message to persevere and look for the silver lining.

With vivid images of the natural world, these poems deal with the dark events we are dealing with. They do not shy away from our challenges. Yet like Jeffrey himself, his poems remain optimistic. They are infused with Christian spirituality. Not that you have to be Christian to love these poems. Somehow Jeffrey has struck a tone that invites religious reflection while also providing a celebration of science and nature. Love and joy in the small wonders!

While I want the readers to experience his poetry fresh, I did want to preview a few lines that struck me. To me they are memorable; while at the same time, encapsulating the lyrical nature of Jeffrey's poems. Here is the first one:

If I met Emily Dickinson I'd ask her to dance

This is simply a fanciful image that I don't think has been created before. I was as surprised at its uniqueness as Dickinson would be at the question.

Here is another memorable line:

I'm thankful for the love and the you and the me

I think so much is said in this line. I like the way Jeffrey connects these three things while also giving them their own space.

Yet another line of Jeffrey's that struck me is:

If life were a Hallmark movie I wouldn't be sad

This line gave me food for thought. Not to knock escapism movies, but Hallmark movies have protagonists that are not facing huge terrible problems. They have problems that are solved in 3 acts. How often do we make our problems bigger than they are? Instead of being miserable, we should find things to be grateful about.

In Jeffrey's poem titled "Jesus" he gives us some thoughts to consider. He asks two bold questions in the same vein as the Beatles "Imagine."

What if Jesus believed in science

. . . . . .

why not rewrite the Bible to reflect a logical mind

. . . . .

Heady stuff doing poetry's intended purpose. Give the poet and the audience a chance to reflect and look at things in a new way. Even if these lines may shock you and you disagree, they are not questions to turn people away from religion but to think about God.

For me, Jeffrey's work touched on my own faith. I have never considered these ideas until I came across them (the best lines in poetry give us new perspectives to consider), but it did make me ponder and consider: Is the New Testament really just a rewriting of the Bible to reflect changing times? Is it time to be rewritten again? Not that I have figured out an answer to these questions, but they are a part of the dialogue we should have about religion.

Jeffrey's collection of poems encapsulates 2021. It helps us deal with the pandemic, the divisiveness, the isolation, and the heartache of our modern lives. Jeffrey reminds us of the beauty and the love that persists despite all our hardships.

In 2021, I was named the first Poet Laureate of Oshkosh. So I write, read, and enjoy poetry. Yet I would not take on this huge challenge that Jeffrey has pulled off. So I tip my hat off to this book. It proves that to get a homerun; you have to take a big swing.

Enjoy this book and help Jeffrey out by visiting his website and leaving reviews where you can.

Thomas Cannon
Poet Laureate of Oshkosh
March 15, 2022

Introduction

It was January 11th, 2021, an icy but sunny winter morning. Our country had just endured an attempted insurrection 5 days earlier, which left much of the world in shock and perhaps in an altered state of pandemonium. After working from home for 9 months I had put on far too many pounds and was feeling depressed and angry. I was 61 years-old and I had less enthusiasm for life in general as I could feel my health deteriorating. I needed goals and motivation, urgently. My wife and I made a serious pledge that day to lose weight in 2021 by dramatically reducing portion size and increasing physical activity. So, I had a solid goal in place that would improve my physical well-being, but how about an intellectual challenge? How about writing a poem a day for a whole year? There is no way, I thought. More realistically, 100 poems in the year might be a more practical goal. Could it be done? I was also thinking of the author Nina Sankovitch who I admire greatly, who fulfilled her goal of reading one book per day and chronicled it in her work "Tolstoy and the Purple Chair." A new personal poetry goal like mine could help motivate members of my local writer's club, The Wordsmiths.

Throughout the year, I was sharing my latest poems with my club, getting some good feedback along the way. It was a fascinating journey as I ended up writing about nature, politics, love, relationships, music, etc. During the year, I also voraciously consumed many of the works of the great poets, like Walt Whitman, William Wordsworth, Robert Frost, Maya Angelou, Edgar Allan Poe, Emily Dickinson, Langston Hughes, and the list goes on. I also would read three excellent short poetry compilations, "Island Verse" by William H. Olson, "Wisconsin Time" by Thomas Cannon, and "Behind the Plow" by Stanley C. F. Hayes, and was quickly gaining confidence that I could finish 100 poems in one year. Later in the year I would be introduced to the works of the late Wisconsin poet, Paul Christy, who is now one of my favorite writers. I know it's a cliché, but once I started writing these poems, it became a labor of love.

As of November of 2021 and I had written about 70 poems. I was thrilled to find out about a poetry open mic to be held in Oshkosh at a place called Planet Perk. I was overjoyed as the crowd showed their appreciation with significant applause in response to my work. I was also very happy to learn about the city of Oshkosh starting a Poet Laureate program. Tom Cannon was named the first Oshkosh Poet Laureate. Cannon, an English major in college, co-organizer of the Oshkosh-based Lakefly Writers Conference, and host of a local cable TV show that interviews writers, read my first 50 poems and he seemed to like the collection and the poetic direction I was going in.

My all-consuming obsession with writing poetry even motivated some friends at work. My friend Erind even starting writing his own poetry, close to 15 poems, after hearing about my project during our noontime walks. Then Bruce and Heather followed suit, with their own writing goals. I think I started something. It was a ripple effect that was more than interesting. At the time of writing this introduction, I was checking into the possibility of starting a poet laureate program in my community of North Fond du Lac.

Until recently, I was having real difficulty trying to name my new book of poems. It was a friend on Twitter and former Wisconsin Poet Laureate Margaret Rozga who suggested, "Maybe you could find the title in a line from the last poem in your collection." Fascinating idea. I found a line from my 100th poem entitled "Transition", the last line as a matter of fact, "And your love still sets my heart at ease." Margaret said, "Why don't you just name it "My Heart At Ease?" The name was born. I knew instantly that was it. When I'm writing at my best, my heart is truly at ease.

Back to the year 2021. January 11th was a sunny day, a high of about 5-degrees. We were in the grips of a nasty and snowy Wisconsin winter. As I gazed out of my back window, I was listening to a song called "Drift Away" by the great Dobie Gray. That gorgeous song gave me the first poem in my collection. I hope you enjoy my work as much as I enjoyed creating it. Feel free to email me at jeffreycmcandrew@gmail.com and tell me what your favorite poem is and why. I would love to hear from you. On Twitter, I'm at @numinous2019. Numinous is the name of my latest novel. It's about a Lutheran minister who has questions about his faith. My author website is jeffreymcandrew.wordpress.com.

TABLE OF CONTENTS

Dobie Gray

Dobie Gray morning, coffee with cream, smell of pumpkin bread
baking, mellowness dominates the morning
Love and freedom and hope and all of that is good in the cocoon of
my morning renewal
I'm lost in the beat, drifting away, encased in the security of music
No more troubled mind, no more heartache, just Dobie and I safe
at home
Snow is settled in the peace of a 5-degree morning, smoke billowing
from chimneys
Peering through the screen door, a black and gray cat outside wants in
He is asking me to feed him. He wants part of my Dobie peace.
No coronavirus, no racial war, no uneasiness can break through
this peace
No angst, no pain, no disapproval, no judgement can pierce my
morning
No argument, no shouting, no confusion and no trouble in life now
No strain on the mind or the body, just Dobie and I in present tense
During this moment in time, I suddenly understand the things I do
more clearly
The blowing snow quickens its pace, a pure white blanket on the
ground is thickening
I now understand that peace of mind can be achieved anytime, and in
any place.

The Vastness

New views of pristine beauty, past the false faces of the crowd, past the undimmed switch of reality
I'm on the pinnacle, in the light, not vulnerable to the "no" the "why not" or the denial of solutions
A river rushes below, and fills my soul like a mindful current unfulfilled, and a light unheeded
Nature's beauty, and this wisdom of time exist, clouded yet clear

Circumstantial evidence not clear but knowing the existence of more
To see more than what can be seen, meeting the challenge, grasping at sublime frequencies
Trudging through this forest of time and place, knowing some but not knowing most
Brief period of time for one life, but intimately connected to all lives, to all life.

Pausing on my walk I see the owl in the tree. Is he looking at me?
From his gaze I sense that he may know a secret that is a part of the eternal glee
Existential mindfulness of nature is present, but there is a feeling of desperation and deficiency that lingers
Vastness of space, gushing of potential, abundance of grace, and a love bomb of emotion.
The owl's stare delivers a revelation of truth and love all at the same time, directly from the heart of nature.

I Know You Feel Lost

I know you feel lost, I know you feel cheated
I know you feel alone I know you feel defeated
What was once you is now gone but you sing your own song
You've lost your sense of purpose but you certainly can't be wrong

You look up into the sky you're probably wondering why
all your days turn into a dark night and fail to take flight

I know you feel lost, I know you feel cheated
You've lost the real you and you feel so damn defeated
What have you got to say when you have nothing left to play
And your bare arms reach out in mourning for a life so forlorning

And wasn't it you that I met before as you fell onto the floor
Grasping tightly at the life that you hid behind the door
Go toward the light my friend and follow your heart
Because this is the best and only way to make your start

Follow

Follow the muse, follow your heart
Follow the trail right from the start
Follow the wise words, don't lose your head
You'll be better off that way, better than dead

Strange music provokes you but can't contain you
The world outside crumbling, much to pay heed to
Reasons for being existing in the light
Know the wise ways and always know what's right

Field and stream and pond and river
Nature's way does give me a shiver
Always in the mood to really know why
Youth dream fading, I say with a sigh

Trouble in Paradise

crumbling country caught in a storm
crying families are becoming the norm
Washington DC in such alarming disarray
waiting for the moment for the night to turn to day

careless moments even for a couple in love
as they huddle together below and above
national breakdown hitting the streets
the Civil War feelings are real, why be discreet?

long ago and far away, I dreamt about a world today
full of love full of peace full of memories that do not cease
full of you and full of me now finally we can see
the beauty of the day, where nothing gets in our way

Dark Days Ahead

Dark and dreary days, hope for the future seems to be waning
Dark forecasts for the human race, violence at the capitol draining
A battle between two different world views, conceptions of freedom differ greatly
A president inciting trouble, is truly unprecedented. Why all of this lately?

Is Trump derangement a syndrome or is it reality perceived?
Dysfunction is the norm and there could be more to grieve?
More what? Greater chaos? What is the purpose of all of this?
Why does this happen in our USA, our precious oasis?

Why does it have to be this way?
The battles in the streets increasing night and day.
People sick with Covid are finding more reasons to be scared
Fears, irrational thoughts and conspiracy laid to bare

Democracy crumbling at its foundation it seems
Are there more hopes for the American dream?
Trying to find the good day by day, hour by hour
But the evidence is showing it's sweet turned sour

Jesus was right. Love is the answer. Love one another.

Strange Days

Physical restrictions and Covid-19 rules aren't restrictions
The mind is still free to love, to think, and to dream
A pandemic's threat, the rumble of the problematic storm shouldn't scare
Civil unrest and negativity could go anywhere
But glass always half-full, always trudging ahead
Be brave for your sons, daughters, mothers, and fathers instead

It's not a normal time, but can be a time of opportunity
Time to refocus on the important things and treasures aplenty
Time to assess friendships
Time to do and say the important things
Time to forge ahead with the help of angels' wings

Plan of action, plan of productivity? What's your plan?
How do you make your perfect stand?
Write that great novel, paint that great painting, or write that new song
Or form that new relationship
In order to gain a better grip

Learn how to better grow the precious flowers around you
Dream bigger, dream humungous, dream on a world scale
Find your peaceful place, do a favor for a friend
See the beauty and truth that never ends
See the potential all around you and weep
See that most of the love in the world is asleep
Be the light in chaos
When all is on fire around us

Be the one who says there is hope
Be the one who says there is love
Be the one who says there is truth
Be the one demonstrating how to live

It's only the crack that lets the light get through.
Yes Leonard, these are strange days, indeed.

Just In Time

Will I find myself just in time to see the morning sun?
Will I find myself just in time to see the joy and fun?
Will I find myself just in time to realize my youth?
Will I find myself just in time to prove what I need to prove?
Will I find myself just in time to seek the light of day?
Will I find myself just in time to look the other way?
Will I find myself just in time to see the world end?
Will I find myself just in time to feel the overall trend?
Will I find myself just in time to see my soul brand new?
Will I find myself just in time to see the real you?
Will I find myself in morning sun where nobody walks away?
Will I find myself in the cheerful morning where we eat, dream
and play?

Precious Time and Hope

precious time races by as the clock tells us it's time
it's time for now, it is time for us, it is time for love
and it is time for truth

precious time tells us what's true and what matters
we imagine the moment in the beautiful package of now

what's past is past, the future is just a dream
it's the present moment with friends held in high esteem

time is of the essence but we are attached to the fabric of HOPE
HOPE never loses momentum, HOPE never pauses to hesitate and
HOPE never gives up
HOPE is connected with FAITH
dear HOPE, I love you all of the time, not just some of the time

Lead With Love

lead with love not hate or hesitation
lead with the heart without reservation
lead with the best part of yourself
with vim, vigor and spiritual wealth

aging prophesy, knowledge of mind
what on Earth am I willing to find?
grandeur of life, planet of beauty
survival comes with faith and duty

lead with your mind but focused on the love
continual battle between the hawk and the dove
lead with the love that is so close at hand
so that others following will understand

Terrible War

Sending young men to fight and die
Killing children in the night
Chaos, and death on the ground
Chilling bombs, crazy sights and sounds
The world is in peril until it changes its ways
When will there be peace today?
Tanks roar and buildings crumble
The stomach of my soul is beyond the rumble
Why scare so many innocent people?
Why destroy the church and its steeple?
We need to care more about our fellow man
Why not advocate for love, to care and understand?
Maybe our purpose on Earth is to say
That there may be more a humane way
To respect all of the planet's life
We must curb the angst, it cuts like a knife
Dylan said the answer is blowing in the wind
No nuclear winter, portending life's end
Leaders like Confucious, Christ or Gandhi needed
So necessary lessons of pacification are heeded
Go where love goes young man
It's your job to understand
The changes needed for the human race
Violent instincts we must erase.
Mankind has a choice to live or perish
Precious future at stake, that we love and cherish
No more time to hesitate or stall
Climb morality's stairs one and all

I Gazed At The Trees

I gazed at the trees on the golden hill
Billowing soft beauty, giving me a thrill
I saw the trees of green brilliant in the light
I tried to hold back tears, with all of my might

The beauty of the Earth is so very true
Each of us perceiving a different hue
Welcome to the party, welcome to the dance
Life engaging life, surely more than chance

The blue sky and the clouds like cotton strands
Here is the wonder and I hold it in my hands
Hands of freedom and hands of love
Hands to create, hands directly above

Here is the lesson I learned today
It's about love and truth on brilliant display
It's all about a miracle one might proclaim
Experience never so different, never quite the same

Struggle

Full of fear, full of doubt
Full of ins, full of out
Looking at you looking at me
Seeing what I'm not supposed to see

Family friction and every day strife
Clinging and wishing for a better life
Why so constrained and why so blue
Trying to find the colorful you

Mighty struggle in this mortal coil
Age's death grip drives us to the soil
A lifetime can make a dreadful mess
Some search for more, some search for less

Reach out cause it's not too late
To find one's passions one should not abate
Meaning carved out of our finite lives
Help me great spirit, make me fly

Mellifluous Words

Mellifluous words flow through the air
Bringing me calm, hours without care
Mellifluous words in good taste
Quiet peace, without haste

What's wrong with the world today
While we work, work, work away
Finding not a calm moment to pause
Finding instead routines, rules and laws

Mellifluous words stated with ease
Calming voices in the summer breeze
Blocking out the world's warlike ways
Satisfying the soul during our dark days

Just As You Are

Debbie just as you are you are my shining star
Always there to talk with wherever you are
Decent, concerned and kind
Without you I would be out of my mind

There will be battles ahead we will fight
United together with all of our might
Helping each other all the way through
The Jeff Deb Team, the sacred two

Through thick and thin and pain and strife
I would entrust you with my life
Forever friends and lovers indeed
Being with you is all I need.

Struggle of Man

Where does this come from?
This certainty without knowledge
This Dunning-Kruger effect of the ego
What makes men and women divide by left and right?

What makes our soul so dark we cannot see?
What focuses on the outside instead of you and me?
What worries us deep within?
Where do we go now and where to begin?

Translucent focus but a need to be transparent
Walking the path but never the errant
Seeking to fight and seeking to see
The truth, hope and light of the real me

I Find Beauty

I find beauty in the passing days
I find beauty in your winsome ways
I find beauty in passers by
I find beauty in you and I

I find beauty in a peaceful stream
I find beauty in your eyes that gleam
I find beauty in your wistful ways
I find beauty in all of our days

I can't stop thinking it's true
The best for me is always you.

Advice For A Friend

Maintain your magic whatever the cost
Inner and outer or else it is lost
Discover the friendships that make you feel good inside
Paint them with love and kindness and even pride

Notice the little things that come from within
See the danger signs before trouble begins
Know the words to say, and which ones to save
It's only you and your actions, you will need to be brave

Feel like the lucky one, the fortunate one indeed
Know the positivity and know to plant the seed
Far more often one should reach out for greatness
Rather than sink into the trap of short-sightedness

What Is This Life?

What is this life that I hold in my hand?
It allows me to fall or to make a stand
What is this life that helps me see?
The real you, the real me

What is this air I breathe?
The moment vulnerable to seize
What allows me to interact?
To add rather than subtract

What makes it fun to do certain things?
To goof around or pursue solemn searchings
What makes it more than grand?
To want only to hold your hand

What is this life that allows me to love?
To gather the prize and partake of
To see the wisdom of the ages
To discover where the power of the heart rages

Last Breath

Bye bye birds bye bye nest
Bye bye what I love the best
Bye bye you bye bye me
Bye bye all I have to see

Bye bye voice bye bye song
Bye bye our chance to get along
Bye bye wisdom bye bye truth
Hello dark age bye bye youth

Bye bye words bye bye air
I guess we won't get anywhere
Bye bye trees bye bye grass
First thing I see might be the last

Glad I had you and a morning song
I love the way we got along
We'll meet again sometime I guess
I found love more and surely not less

There's a place I long to see
It's full of you and full of me
Distant starlight Sunday best
Our story's there, you know the rest

It Fills My Mind

Like a gentle breeze it comes
Whispering on the wind it comes
Like a gentle breeze it comes
It fills my mind, it fills my mind

Like birds in summer
Hushed voices in springtime
I hold you tight
Falling in love, falling in love

Like you and I
We find our way home
Like you and I
We find our way home, find our way home

Like a summer breeze it comes
Like you and I
Like a summer breeze it comes
It fills my mind, fills my mind

Like you and I
Our love shows all the time
Like you and I
You fill my mind you fill my mind

Memorial (for Stef)

I see your face over and over again
I cannot pretend you're not here
I wait for a sign, or a notification
I'm patient for our souls to persevere

Sitting in my home waiting for your call
Sitting here wondering if I'll ever hear anything new
Scared out of my wits, waiting for my spirits to fall
Chasing out the bad thoughts, chasing out the blues

Thinking about your humor and your special grace
Thinking about the time you made me laugh so hard
Thinking about the time you put me in my place
Wondering why fate would play this cruel card

That's life I guess it is true
I cannot chase the blues away about you
I cannot sit and stare in space
But I know you're with me, spirit, time and place

There's So Much

There's so much love in my heart today
There's so much love in this game we play
There's so much love in the you and the me
There's so much love in the future we see

There's so much light and the grass is green
There's so much hope more than can be seen
There's so much light in this world which is round
There's so much goodness in taste, sight and sound

There's so much grace in that which we call we
As we carry each other to eternity
There's so much joy for me and you
There's so much great work for us to do

Praise

Praise of sunshine praise of dew
Praise of the new day praise of you
Praise of hearts who are held so true
Praise of the cracks of light, pushing through

Praise for justice praise for peace
Praise for the good things done in the least
Praise for highlights praise for the moon
Praise for everlasting coming our way soon

Praise for you and praise for me
Praise for the world that's meant to be
Praise for rivers, streams and lakes
Praise for your love which I will never forsake

Praise for highways, byways and rustling winds
Praise the love between next of kin
Praise for summer, spring, winter and fall
Praise for the courage to go for it all

Unknown Reality

Somersaults into the unknown reality
Graceful time exists for all
Finding ways to parachute
Into the ideal disastrous fall

Finding time to find ways to think
But not too deep not too far to sink
Troubled times troubled lot
Traveling into the time forgot

Peaceful ways and finding the time
Expressing myself with ample rhyme
Travel the pathway to the less than normal
Weaving my way to the perfect informal

Fears of the new shoved into the past
To a brave new world that surely will not last
Human dreams and close connections stay
Pushing moral impediments out of the way

Time is Precious

Hoping and dreaming our wishes come true
Hoping you love what I love about you
Waiting and trying for the next time
So proud of why I'm feeling so fine

Can't understand why we can't live forever
Can't pursue every path and endeavor
Saying the right words make them come through
It's all I have to say and it's all about you

Can't remember when I didn't love you all the time
Compassion isn't silly, happiness is not a crime
Wishes dreams and hopes surely do come true
It's like we both wanted and all I want is you

Billowing Beauty

Billowing willows in my backyard
Beauty evident I cannot disregard
Picturesque scenery obvious to the awake
Waiting for the gorgeous picture I will take

What have I discovered on my own turf
A silence, grace and nature unearthed
Still waters of my soul discover comfort in shade
Thankful for the graceful presence it has made

Greenness captured in July's essence
Walden's inspiration and many life lessons
Drinking up mother nature in a dream I'm told
Revitalizing my spirit, a pleasure filled with gold

Thinking About Our Song

Listening to Van Morrison, Sunday morning, coffee cup full of love
Searching, observant to the penetrating universe above
Spellbound by beauty of the melody and the sublime point of view
Mesmerized... have I told you lately that I love you?

Peace days and strength, simple and profound
You fill my heart with gladness, baby I want you around
Frame of mind quite sublime and true
Ease my troubles is what you do

Getting back to basics of your grace
Listening and touching your loving place
Reaching to the highest height
Bright future, our togetherness takes flight

Let's listen to our song the rest of our days
New dreams and potential beautifully ablaze
I like when I can talk to you about my hopes
And we cheerfully climb love's amazing slopes

My love is strong, true and right
I picked you in 1993 at the first sight
Sweet and rare as Tupelo honey
Your soulful love, greater than money

Scary Dream

mean shadows on the wall of my room
unsightly dreams bringing such doom
one could lash out at such extreme fright
tossing and turning for the rest of the night

goblins here and everywhere in sight
ghosts reflecting strange beams of light
my worries turn ugly as I awake in a sweat
never denying the ever-present scent of death

bloodcurdling reality is ever present here
ship of insanity, no captain to steer
no rainbows of luck, dark visions creep
into the night of limitless and frightening sleep

could there be an answer to this darkness?
this reeling confusion, no one to stand with
is it real, contrived or something in-between?
the soul tells me the answer in a dream

Sitting On The Back Porch

Melody in my ear, classical and artful sound
Tommy Emmanuel Beatles tune, I'm springtime bound
Witnessing the birds and the budding, happy trees
Robins play love songs in the early morning breeze

World shows me how it's brand new
Giving the angels what they are due
Sometimes in the morning light
We live with zest and forget the fright

Grim and long shadows from the trees
But no anger and angst here please
Take your troubles to another place
Because I'm here to enjoy nature's pure grace

Leonard's Courage

I'm going to go out like Leonard Cohen
Facing love and truth and poetry until the end
I'm going to go out like the master
With all of my compassion to send

I'm going to go out like the man
Who fights with powerful verse in hand
Who makes an artistic stand
Who always has a plan

Dancing until the end of love
With our evolving souls in flame
Thunder and lightning above
What happens to the heart is not the same

Rage against the dying of the light
Remember youths magic, and suffering is might
Cradle the innocent, but hurdling towards the dark
Life is not a game, it's really quite an art

You Create Love

You create love
You create peace
You are the loving thing
And you do it with ease

Your smile makes me laugh
And you do it all the time
You take me to my happy place
And you make it all rhyme

I was walkin' down the path of love one day I said look at that love,
I like it that way.
It's hard to be pessimist when you look at the light because the life
is comin' in with all of its might
People tryin' to tell me life is so wrong but when I look at your smile
I start my own song.
People tryin' to tell me life is so wrong but when I look at your smile
I start my own song.

Take It

Take it onward and upward
Take it all the way
Take the loving spirit
Take it all day

Take it with you when you leave
Take it while you drive
Take it when you grieve
Take it while you're alive

Take it when you're here and there
Take it when you're everywhere
Take it with you traveling home
Take it when you're all alone

Take it all of the time
Take it and make it fine
Take it when you leave home
Take it wherever you roam

Take it to the limit
Take more than you give it
Take it with when you die
Take it instead of asking why

Take it with a friend
Take it with a foe
Take it with interest
Take it wherever you go

Turn

Turn down the noise turn down the hype
Turn down the fake, turn down the gripe
Turn up the joy, turn up the grace
Turn on the life, put a smile on your face

Show your friends some effort, show them some compassion
Show them what you feel, show them real fashion
Show them what you know, show them how you feel
Show them what is loving, truthful and real

Turn down the violence, turn down the tragic
Turn down the negative, make your own magic
Turn on the lights, show the real you
Turn on the lights, you see what you have to do

Hedges Road

don't take me down Hedges Road
where the crab grass grows with no boundaries
and the weeds live where they want to
where the fences are all tattered

don't take me down Hedges Road
where the country is mocked and dreams explode
don't take me down the rugged and rough way
because my soul is smooth and completely unfrayed

don't take me down Hedges Road
where dreams are sparse and troubles unload
don't take me down Hedges Road
where ego is king and morals erode

don't take me down Hedges Road
where the left tire is flat and common sense corrodes
don't take me down Hedges Road
where chaos reigns and expectations are low

there is a better road

There's a New Cat in the Neighborhood

there's a new cat in the neighborhood and his name is John
he won't be kind he won't be here for long
he'll marry another and make new friends
we'll wait and see how this sad story ends

he'll prance and posture and play the friend game
until one by one they find his empathy lame
all practiced and polished he will swindle you dry
his life is all a show, his whole life a lie

there's a new cat in neighborhood and his game is rough
you must stand your ground you must call his bluff
he's bad to the bone and will hurt all in his way
make a beeline for the door because he's bound to stay

there's a new cat in town and he's playing for keeps
he plays with emotions and cares not who weeps
please fly away, cause this man will do you harm
no substance, just anger and all he has is charm

dear Lord I hope Jesus is with you today
because this feral feline is ready and willing to play

Heaven

i'm traveling to the end of the sun
where victories are seen and dreams are won
i'm traveling to the end of the sun
where celebration takes place and songs are sung

i'm traveling to the end of the earth
where wings fly high and newness gives birth
i'm traveling to the end of the now
i'm not sure about where, when or how

i'm traveling to the end of time
where there is no fear and spirit does climb
i'm traveling to the end of the streets
where hearts are satisfied and dreams complete

i'm traveling to the end of love
where beauty persists and always above
i'm traveling across the rainbow skies
where there are no falsehoods or lies

i'm traveling to the perfect peace
where my heart lies calm and pain does cease
i'm traveling to the perfect place
pointing towards the light, where souls embrace

Fleeting Time

As years go by life has more meaning
Do we simply exist or is it all dreaming
The cascade of days flow smoothly by
As I look to the world I wonder why

Slow fading life held in my hand
All the commotion and trouble I barely understand
Take a whiff of courage and might and will
See the earth so beautiful so incredibly still

I'm puzzled at the infinity of time
Life is so short but so wonderfully sublime
Existence is good in most of its ways
Humans scrambling for purpose most of their days

Where is my here and where is my now
But mostly I'm wondering why and how
How do I make my case in point
Pondering which of God's wonders to anoint

Cheerful expression, look of love
Less like the hawk, more like the dove
Wandering endlessly in nature's grace
Finding my best effort, time and place

Rachael

You passed on a beautiful and warm summer day
Rachael, you breath of fresh air, surrounded by love
Cancer robbed you of later years
Conjured up all kinds of fears
But you met it with grace and courage on that warm summer day

The Eiffel Tower, Air Supply, creativity and giving
Your smile encouraged us all to live our best living
Spending time with you was always worthwhile
Our sorrow so deep, you walked the extra mile

Rachael graceful, Rachael true
What are we now to do?
Your life has passed but always in our hearts
Without you we must make a new start

We see her beautiful soul now,
We see it in plain view
We see the tears on the faces
We see the love shining through

We comfort each other with grace, hope and love
Remembering Rachael as she soars above
Bright and vibrant colors to remember you by
You touched our Earth, you touched our sky

Please say a prayer for Rachael tonight
As she soars above, an angel in flight
A caring mother, children now on their own
Her spirit is still here and we're never alone

Poem 40

This is Poem 40 and what do I write?
Something heavy or something light?
What subject do I think about today?
Where is the source and it goes which way?

Where is the muse I love so much?
To love, to think about and to touch.
Where is the way through the dark enchanted woods?
As a brave poet, how do I deliver the goods?

There must be a path to the clearing
Is it me or is it God steering?
Many thoughts in my head at once
Always with challenges on many fronts

So as I put my pen to paper today I just have to say
Will the muse leave or will he stay?
I've got to find one way to express
The great more and not the empty less.

Death

what is death? darkness and no more?
or is there something extra at the core?
is there a soul that survives?
or is that something humans contrive?

what's it like to not exist?
no laughter, crying...no more clenched fist
what's it like to not be?
no time and no future to see

tell me it's OK, tell me it's perfect peace
tell me all the pain and all the trouble does cease
tell me life continues in some form
tell me there's a way out of the storm

It comes down to you and me
living is what you make it you see
life's colorful canvass will come to an end
but it's never over for you and me my friend

Bold Is The Only Way

Don't go through life shyly
Don't think about doing it mildly
Give it your best shot
Might as well, and why not?

The beauty ahead makes life sweet
Like the multi-colored flowers we often meet
The sweet tasting wine of friends and song
Shows us that we really belong

Why drift by when we can focus on the goal
To be not an empty vessel but a brilliant soul
I see loved ones being gay and enjoying the laughs
But are they really living before their last gasps?

Who knows what time has in store
Hopefully there's much, much more
But if we don't try will never know
Time to dive head first into the show

Stormy College Reunion

Stormy night, on the porch at Hughes Hall
Nostalgia for one and surely for all
Sharing stories and belly laughs
Even enjoying the most outrageous gaffes

As the night roars we think about our precious time
How we are lucky to be here and the clock does chime
Gratitude for everything that is gone now and missed
Sweetness and sadness commonly coexist

This freedom on the porch focusing on the now
As we have traveled further than many are allowed
The storm a reminder of how we must prize
The life that goes like lightening before all of our eyes

The Mystery

A virus here, a virus there, a virus seems to be everywhere
A symptom here, a symptom there requiring traveling with
extreme care
Deepest mystery, a new paradigm of science?
Causing us to question our own self-reliance

Will the variants ever stop or do we stay petrified in fear?
Scared to go far and scared to go near
How much longer will this breakout last?
Afraid of the future, clinging to the past

How safe are the vaccines? the petrified cry
Is it science or is it all a big lie?
We can stand together and fight or divided we fall
We have to find the answer or it's tough times for all

Peacemaker's Lament

Oh I wish war was gone
Oh I had heard it could be destroyed
Give it the boot, sing it its final song
So nobody has to be angry and annoyed

Get rid of the anger get rid of the strife
Get rid of arguments that stand-in the way
Let people live a better life
This is what I have to say

Convert indifference to love
Shout to the heavens above
War you're not welcome any more
Greet compassion, show hate the door

It may take a long time
To get rid of the murder and the crime
Trouble could raise its ugly head
Or will we experience tranquility instead?

Careful Ways

The way to work is soft not hard
Planning gently to make a new start
Careful not to miss the right way
Stirring the waters not too much today

Casual dreaming nonchalant view
Helping and caring and feeling deeply for you
Nothing lost in avoiding careless ways
In doing this, there's nothing more to say

Good things come to those who wait
Not worrying about being a little late
Not fretting much about the big frantic pace
Because the tortoise usually wins the race

I Have

I have the choice to do what's right
I have the choice to use all my might
I have the choice to be alone
I have the choice to set the tone

I have the will to try very hard
I have the will to make a good start
I have the will to change my views
I have the will to see a new you

I have a chance to touch the sky
I have a need to wonder why
I have the right to be number one
I have the courage to see that it's done

Far and Wide

If you care to dream whatever you will
A stagnant life will not stay still
if you travel somewhere in the day
Make sure the colorful story goes your way

If you would make a cheerful new friend
You may not know where the journey will end
Until you reach strong, far and wide
You'll never realize what's inside

An Old Man's Dream

Strange dreams I had last night
I was far away, away from site
The people I met were strange and good
I could say hello in a brand-new neighborhood

Bizarre feelings after my sleep
It wasn't too strong it did not make me weep
Was that my mother holding my hand?
As I entered that uncharted land

Where yesterdays are gone and the future appears
Could this dream be meant to assuage my fears?
Yet there is comfort in the night
As I chase the stars so bright

One More Summer Day

Give me one more summer day
Where the birds sing and sunlight does play
Give me one more peaceful night
Where the crickets chirp in their sublime delight

Give me one more chance at youth
No time misspent, heading toward a final truth
Squinting through the intense light of love
Beautiful sunlight penetrating above

Each day a gift from a higher source
Enjoying each moment, nature sets the course
What I know and proclaim is true
Is what I can and cannot see through

Porch swing night, peace of the gods
You and I together, what are the odds?
Each season is gravy and there is a lot
Each life a great novel, we're lost in the plot

As We Go Down Today

let us go down to the place that we found a place that we found
far away
you can bring trouble and I'll bring his double as we go down today
you think I'm crazy and I think you're lazy as we go down today
oh you think I'm lazy and I think you're crazy as we go down today

let's have it out, let's find the answer today
let's both reach out maybe we can make it a better day
we don't need pain we've suffered enough anyway
all I need is you together we find a better way

let me bring love from the place up above as we go down today
you can bring your brother and I'll bring another as we go
down today
it will all make sense as we find the right defense as we go
down today
you can bring Jesus and I bring my reasons as we go down today

let's have it out, let's find the answer today
let's both reach out maybe we can make it a better day
we don't need pain we've suffered enough anyway
all I need is you together we find a better way

We can bring love from that place up above as we go down today
We can bring love from that place up above as we go down today

Broken Man

There was an old man and his name was Jess
He might've done what he cannot confess
Thinkin' about the life he might've lived
Strange how it seems it all goes through the sieve

A failed life and a writer by trade
What happened to all the plans he made?
Tried to strike it rich, tried to be a saint
Cryin' and shoutin' about the man he ain't

Speaking out at the top of his lungs
Tears abound about the song not sung
Furious night, the past won't rescue him
Quite disturbing, the way he now lives

He's a broken man through and through
What else is he supposed to do?
His heart is aching all of the time
Never found love and the sun don't shine

The End of Summer

Desperate sunlight wrapping on my window pain
Last days of summer are here again
Days are waning and night takes over
into the cold dark hands of October

As September takes its last breath
Trees and flowers bravely face their death
I'm not fond of fall it truly does seem
Because warmth leaves, it's the end of the gleam

Joy, oh joy where are you now?
Can you tell by my weathered brow?
Hope seems lost and new dreams seem distant
But love struggles to stay alive in every instant

The Fates

No one knows when the fates will sway
Gather ye rose buds while ye may
Feeling the grip of time's icy hand
I struggle and stumble to take a stand

What's in store after we die?
Living in life's memories we try and try
It slips away it evaporates dry
It leaves us anxiously wondering why

Oh fate tell me where I stand today
Tell me the answer where fears allay
Tell me how to think, jump and play
Love and truth show me the way

The road may be long, scary and deep
But without risk what will I reap?
I see the stunning sun setting off in the west
Will I have courage to face the rest?

Each faces the unknown in different ways
Within a poignant and ravishing haze
Precious time evaporates by the hour
As we see which demons we need to devour

Let our souls be a candle in the dark
In the cave, a hopeful spark
Know all that you can become
Until the day's work is done

Loving Fall

Beautiful morning orange are the trees
The fallen leaves give soft repose
I wait on the soft edge of being
as the summer slowly goes

Where is the brilliant sunlight now?
The kind I wished for somewhere somehow
Golden leaves fall all around me
Destiny calls nature astounds me

With deep breaths of life
Comes continuing strife
Eventually we all fall down
But hope comes through solid and sound

The crunching of leaves the smell of hot apple cider
The cool breeze in my face makes my soul all the lighter

Cold reminder of the cycle of life
But good memories can persist so ever ripe
Breath is visible at first October's dawn
Leaves fall gently on this peaceful morning lawn

Face the cold with courage and glee
The dying of the light is no place for me
The leaves will fall and some tears too
As we trudge through time, me and you

Corporate Stalemate

The hours turn to days to months to years
In the hamster's wheel I try to steer
Working with no end in sight
Manufacturing direction with all of my might

It's strange to be treading water
When competition gets meaner and hotter
When the rigors of the job get more intense
Seems I'm always looking over the fence

Days have some meaning but purpose needs fulfilling
Is it my very healthy soul I'm killing?
Let's stop and think today
How much is me and how much is they?

The Wall

I tried to find the answer but stumbled behind the wall
I got tired of choosing and decided to gently fall
Never mind the losing
I just got tired of it all

Wind pressed against my cheeks
Howling of the ages
Sometimes the future looks grim
As I continue to turn the pages

Life experienced was well lived
Facing the future with grace
Who knows what's left in me
As youth flees without a trace

Love In Your Heart

Do you know love in your heart?
Or do you just know how to play your part?
Do you cover yourself in laughter?
Or do you camouflage forever after?

Do the stains on the windowsill represent your soul?
Or is it the light coming in that your eyes behold?
Is your face hiding cold and repressed rage?
Or with forgiveness will you turn the page?

I can't completely figure you out my friend
It's possible this doubt will never end
But when I see your relaxed smile I know
The beauty you're truly intending to show

Old

As we lose our abilities we gain appreciation…
For the things we have
As we grow old we remember times when everything worked
And the mind was sharp, exuding curiosity

The sad thing is they all go…body, spirit and mind
The aging process is not always kind
We live our life one day at a time
As we fade further away from our prime

But please don't worry and don't fret

One great life is all we get

More

You have one shot make it count
You have one life make it shine
Have a purpose without a doubt
Find a road you can call "mine."

Go for a thrill go for a ride
See what is truly inside
Aim to play fair aim to play clean
Be the greatest person ever seen

Learn to jump learn to fly
Never bother asking why
Treasure the moment truly be blessed
Understand the more and not the less

There Is More Love Left

Desperation in the air
desperation everywhere
When will we get it right?
trying with all of our might

Time gets shorter and care gets greater
fuels the soul sooner rather than later
existence is short, love all we can
The spiritual kind before time began

look to the light look up above
It's gentle and precious as a graceful dove

look to the west look to the east
look for the soul's value to increase
look real close and look real deep
the secrets to treasure, the answers to keep

Dad

Frozen in time
Dad crystallizes memories of mine
Sitting in this waiting room thinking of him
Wishing for the best but out on a limb

Life not so nice but in him I see hope.
Every indication of yes, no evidence of no.
Stories of love and stories to treasure
Feelings of family, hard to measure

Someday I will walk out into the world without Dad
No doubt that I will be beyond sad
There will be many questions to ponder and to see
But his love and encouragement will always exist in me.

Saving Life

Wide expanses of the universe but I only know my home
Friendly earth, nature's miracles every day show

Show me now, show me the features
Show me how to relate to all of God's creatures
Save the earth, save the sky, save the seas
We cannot accomplish our goal with aimless ease

I have the freedom to play my part
Preserving life — the most esteemed form of art
Stay out of trouble and lead the way
For this grand purpose I must have a say

Love and the World

In years to come the world will become a meaner place
Environment flying out of balance, ethics hardly a trace
There will come a time when mankind is challenged to the hilt
And some will wonder why all this civilization was built

tearing apart is easy but building is difficult and slow
This concept is important for the children to know
The love we express on Earth is key
Even though progress is slow to see

Wading through the tears in my eyes
I see a grand and marvelous surprise
I see future grandchildren anxious to find
A world which is so much more than kind

Hearing Bad News

I can tell by the light coming from your eyes
That emotions flow with no disguise
What you communicate to me
Is the pure essence of what is to be

Telling me this I pause and stare into space
Not noticing time or place
It seeps in slowly and takes affect
Emotions gushing, trying to keep them in check

What has happened has happened I cannot stop fate
The power of the moment I cannot overstate
Many well wishes from my partner in time
Telling me that sadness is surely not a crime

Golden Vacation

I'm going on a vacation
I'm going on a trip
There's going to be elation
It's going to be so hip

You can surely see it in my eyes
The future's golden now, near is the prize

Sitting by the pool and lying in the sun
Fun and enjoyment shared by everyone
Palm trees wave in the distant breeze
In the warmth it's pure joy we seize

Turning 62

what does the future hold?
for one relatively old
who still wants to stay
still learning to play

what's left in this banquet of life?
where youth's edge cuts like a knife
where is the magic that's still here?
where we dream but bravely fear

standing strong, not fearing the reaper
finding compassion I'm my brother's keeper
not staying mired in fear's grip
staying engaged, but apprehensive of the trip

surviving in the cancer of this world
while the winds of confusion do solemnly swirl
locating the essence of the true me
as hope rushes restlessly in the cool breeze

it's my life, time and place
wanting to stay strong in this race
seeing all of the potential still
which lies beyond the next hill

Come What May

If I could kiss the sun I would
I would not hold back
For its one life we have
In dreams there is nothing we lack

If I could touch my dreams I would
Sailing into some wonderful night
Doing what one man could
Striving with all my might

If I could change the past I would
Seeing past potential fluttering in the breeze
Watching different lives pass before me
Achieving my goals with ease

What can I plan, do or say?
To have it more my way
Still waiting for a new day
Piloting the future come what may

Tilted By Prayer

Now tilted in prayer humbled by the river
Awareness now shifts, I am shaken by a shiver
Mesmerized by nature and its powerful current
Knowing the true essence knowing what's urgent

I turn my head to the stars and what do I see
A brilliant display a wonderful tapestry
Moonlight reflects off the river's edge
I'm careful not to step off the ledge

Beauty reigns on this river tonight
As I pause to reflect on this wonderful site
I talk to the sky and question the meaning
Is there a purpose and someone intervening?

Suddenly Something Different

I throw a stone into the pond and ripples make it suddenly
something different
I share a kind word and a friend's world is suddenly something
different
I share a smile and the energy in the room is suddenly something
different.
I take a political stand and it can make society suddenly something
different.

Dancing With Emily Dickinson

If I met Emily Dickinson I'd ask her to dance
I'd ask her a question I would take a chance
I'd ask her how lovely the sky is today
I'd tell her to explain it in her own particular way

I would study the way she would prance about
I would marvel at the way she moved in and moved out
Total access to this gold-plated poet
A treasure in front of me, not even knowing it

I might see myself in her eyes
I can't hold back, there is no disguise
Poetry is the future and the future is bright
I might be wrong but I'm probably right

Beauty Surrounds Me

I want beauty to surround me
Like a lover to hold me
I want beauty to be real
I don't want it to be concealed

I'm looking for a kind things around me
The fruits of my actions will astound me
Searching for the many multitudes of good
Looking to do what I really should

Carefully finding my way to the light
I'm really trying to make it right

Making my way to the promised land
With a strong urge to understand
And the appreciation of me and you
That's all I ever needed to do

Carefully finding my way to the light
I'm really trying to make it right

Darold

You went away too soon
How could I not have had a clue?
That you would be taken so abruptly
It jostled my soul unjustly

You backed me, you taught me, you mentored me
You supported me, you molded me and cared for me
Your moral universe bent toward justice
Islands of genius amongst us

An extraordinary person you were
Hope and knowledge for sure
You were the best for mankind
Exploring the limits of the mind

You cared for all of us
Much more than we could discuss
Dreams of knowledge stay alive
New purposes always thrive

You gave us mellowing as a humble gift
Our souls you did gently uplift
Our hearts hopeful, we learned our own song to sing
Hope for humanity your compassion did bring

Thankful

I'm thankful for the stars and the sun and the rain
And even the pain
I'm thankful for the love and the you and the me
And the ecstasy…of living a life fulfilled

I'm thankful for the smiles I see everywhere
Even for the grayness in my hair
I'm thankful for every moment of life
I'm thankful for my generous wife

I'm thankful for the glass half-full
I'm thankful for the push and pull
I'm thankful for the astounding grace
I see every day in your beautiful face

I'm thankful for the coming together and the unity
And the pieces that go together so beautifully
I am in love with beauty and truth
Getting older but looking back at youth

How we live the rest of our days it seems
Would depend on the power of our dreams
And if we can't fix things today
Our love will be led completely astray

I am thankful for the essence that makes love pure
It's undeniable I'm really sure
Take time to meditate on all you see
It will empower you to reach for eternal glee

Gray Skies

not sunny not cloudy but just plain gray
how do I get the light to come back and stay
which way must I push or pull
to take in the breath of life and make it full

it's not the average day I'm looking for
but a day like I've never seen before
taking stock of what's before me
trying different things that will astound me

don't rain on my parade today gray sky
I want to know where the true essence lies
out of the blue and into the light
i'm not choosing wrong and I'm siding with the right

Wonderful Ryan

Wondering tonight if you're doing all right
My son in the world with a future so bright
Troubles exist and the turbulence is real
I'm experiencing the depth of what a father does feel

You live on your own and decisions are made
A father waits patiently as the best plans are laid
Relationship and job pressures do abound
Hoping that each journey ends safe and sound

Wishing that you work it out all on your own
And wanting you to feel not so alone
Because we all go through these troubles and this strife
Trying to make the best sense out of life.

Here's my thought for you today
That in this troubled world you don't forget to play
Don't lose that childlike gleam in your eye
I love you forever my wonderful Ry

Hand in Hand Forever

(This poem originally appeared in my first book published in 2003
titled "Our Brown-Eyed Boy." I added two verses and reworked
some other details today to reflect some of my latest feelings about my
youngest son Stephen. When I first wrote this poem Stephen was 7
years-old. He is now 25. Lately we have seen more behavioral issues
but we are teaching him hugs again. I am optimistic for the future.)

You take my hand you give me five
I love you and help you survive
hand-in-hand we face the world
A novel to be written a story to be told

when you took your first steps we cried with joy
I was learning, what a treasure what a great boy
you are a person of value for sure
for better or worse or for richer or poorer
you're not a cruel mistake of nature
But a Picasso flower to love and nurture
your playfulness is strong and wise
truth and beauty live deep in your eyes

what does the future hold we ask?
you're an adult now and we are ready for the task
as you grow and change you still need love
hugs from mom and dad you can't get enough of

we love you all the time you know that's true
you're a special son and caring is what we came to do
to help you through life with a guiding hand
hoping our kindness you will always understand

Getting Old with My Love

I feel invested in your love I feel you so close
I feel the bones creak but friendship is always the most
I hear the echoes from your room, help is what you're asking for
We're buckling down, getting ready for what's in store

There is magic in the air
And still a sense that we care
That propels us on and on
Always hoping for another dawn

We both look into the mirror
And we notice we're still here
The youth we saw is gone
But still feel like we belong

The ghost of time echoes through the caverns of our lives
Casting new meaning on every day that arrives
Not afraid of the future but responsible for our past
Enjoying each moment, as we know it will not last

Hope

Hope in the future that golden dream
Positivity is better felt than seen
To have a friend to share events of today
To reinforce hope in what both will say

What's the purpose and key to life?
What would it take to see both sides?
What would the entire answer be?
What is the best direction of life to see?

Are we invested in the purpose of existence?
Or are we to follow the path of less resistance?
Do we know the real answer of the dream?
Or do we only see reality via what can be seen?

So let's have hope about what we do today
That will reinforce the dreams we do and say
Let's help others see the light
To learn what's wrong and what is right

A Visit With Charlie at the Nursing Home

I see Charlie in his nursing home bed
all the things to say and all the things left unsaid
how to choose discourse in the final stages
as his course toward death internally rages

Who's going to fix this moment at hand
when all I truly want to do is understand
I tell him I'm thankful for his friendship and how hard he tries
he presses on the side rails and attempts to rise

I tell him that Christmas spirit is in the air
But to challenge his beliefs I do not dare
He says "Jeffrey I don't believe in such things."
As I turn and leave the nursing home room in tears
He says something to assuage all of my fears
He says "Merry Christmas Jeffrey!"
And I will remember this for all the rest of my years

The Arduous Climb

This rocky and abstract path I walk
Avoiding the noxious, but talking the talk
Climbing the mountain, wind against my face
Making the memories that time cannot erase

I make my stand and fate rages before me
Death and tragedy won't defeat me
I now see the white snowy cap, the end in site
As I trudge through the snow, it's victory's delight

All that I can and ever wanted to be
Remains a major mystery
Pondering the numinous, looking heaven's way
Glancing at the snowy peak, where I will forever stay

A Hallmark World

If life were a Hallmark movie I wouldn't be sad
I would think about all of the good things and always be glad
The man from the city would come and run the Inn
Bliss will be felt and we would grin a big grin

Is it the woman's boyfriend who is secretly a prince?
Or is it the small-town mayor discovering someone to love?
Or is it a miracle that changes all things?
Or new music through the town that eternally rings?

Oh give me Norman Rockwell give me the good ole days
Give me a world without cognitive haze
Give me a place where I can live and play with delight
Give me peace and hot chocolate throughout the night

Though true happiness may be meant for fools
I can glance at a world where contentment does rule
There's no other place I'd rather be
Than in this Hallmark world that I'm thrilled to see

The Table

I found myself rushing to where commotion lives
Sprinting to where the life blood is
Heading to the table as long as I am able
To give what there is to give

Walking the walk and talking the talk
Trying not to get it wrong
Contributing to the conversation in depth
Respecting the length, width and breadth
I'm hearing my own song

Memories

I have such wonderful memories with you

Feeling the sands of the beach in Mexico the grains between our toes
Hearing the whistling of the wind on that warm summer night that
caressed our cheeks
Remembering the bench we both sat on in 1993 when you leaned
on my shoulder
Recalling that day I saw you coming down the aisle glowing with
pride looking at me so lovingly

I remember when we renewed our vows on that pier on the
Caribbean Sea
I think back to when we first made love, and we became lovers and
best friends
I cherish when we told each other we would take care of each other
forever, sickness and in health
Most of all I treasure the truth that marrying you was the best
choice I ever made in my life

I Want to Love

I want to live, want to live, want to live
I want to love, want to love, want to live
Now you know, I want to love
Now you know, I want to love

I want the truth, want the truth, in my life
I want the truth, want the truth, in my life
I want you to know how I'm feeling
I want you to know how I'm feeling

I know you, know you, know you well
I know you, know you well, know you well
Please don't hesitate to be on my side
Please don't hesitate to be on my side

I want the ideal you and the ideal me
Hugging up in a tree
Feel the intense and wonderful glee
For you and me…for you and me

I want to love, want to love, only you
I want to love, only you, only you.

A Painful Duel

The man wondered why he had no friends
No shoulder to cry on, no way to pretend
He wondered why the world was so cruel
Why is being kind was such a painful duel?

Why are social structures so strict?
Why are the windows so narrow and thick?
Why did I pick these friends I picked?
The situation almost makes me sick?

Why does life seem so much like a trap or a prison?
When there's so much positivity to envision
Why must I have to look away from love?
When caring and trust is what I'm made of

Over The Edge

I'm going over the edge
I'm going over the edge
I'm going over the edge for you

I'm living a daring dream
I'm living in between
I'm living a fantasy with you

My future is over the edge
My past is already done
My future is over the edge with you

Sometimes it feels unreal when you smile and say
That you could live on and on with me some way
Sometimes it makes me feel so brand new
When you state calmly, "I love you."

I have feelings over the edge
My life is poetry over the edge
My time is precious and over the edge
With you
With you

Past Dreaming

Past dreaming I knew I was seeking
Past dreaming of you
Past dreaming I knew was thinking of you

Past dreaming I thought I was seeing
Past dreaming of you
Past dreaming I knew I was trying
Past dreaming of you

Past dreaming, I knew I was loving
Past dreaming, my mind kept thinking of you

Past dreaming I knew I was hoping
Past dreaming of you
Past dreaming, my dreams were all centered on you

Past dreaming I knew I was asking
Past dreaming of you
Past dreaming, I know it won't happen again
Past dreaming, I know it won't happen again

Don't You Love Her

Don't you love her when she's mad?
Don't you love her when she throws your life away?
Don't you love her when she's sad?
Don't you love her when she's saying her last goodbye?

Don't you love her when she says?
Love unending and the story never ends?
Don't you love her when she's mean?
Goes through everything that you've ever been?

Don't you love her when she's strong?
Don't you love her when she rights every wrong?
Don't you love her when she loves?
Don't you love her when she loves?
Don't you love her when she loves?

Last Grasp

Sanity's last grasp is by a warm thread
It feels your desperation feels your dread
Walk around weary all the long night
Looking for something to come out right

Heavenly whispers, it's kindness I love
Peace of mind and wellness is all I think of
Grasping at truth, grasping at reason, grasping at faith
Grasping for the love innate
Grasping for the you, grasping for the me
Grasping for all that I can see

Absorbing the loss that hits so strong
With my faith and hope trying to get along
The new days with loss will be hard
Constantly finding a feeling to guard

Without parents new truths will be learned
A brand-new courage will be earned
On into the 60's with less support
Obsession with life being ultrashort

Hiding under the covers will not hide
The troubling feelings I have inside
Thoughts of a beautiful past
Are demolished at last

The Noontime Walkers

If you want to walk the walk and talk the talk
The noontime walkers really rock
They talk about love, work and pain
And sometimes discuss things that are really insane

Keep on the lookout for Bruce, Erind and Jeff
They converse with all the passion they have left
Always eager to face another day
And open to see things in an entirely different way

Conversations

Listening to you talk about your favorite alpha males
Tells me more about your story, it never fails
But I'm always somewhat relieved
To see what a bonding of men achieves

Subjects while on the walk include
Life goals planned plain and true
Never apologetic about what we choose
The genuine me and the genuine you

Seeing each other's dreams rising
Respecting each other, never despising
It's all about the meeting of the souls
Before time says we're far too old

Room 229

In room 229 it was quite sublime
It was hard work and ecstasy
I knew it was always the best time
To show my creativity

It was a goal to realize the reporters dream
Creative writing not always what it seems
Mr. Harrell and his late-night paste-up crew
Never a moment when there wasn't something to do

Scalpone sweating bullets and Evans & Miller in the darkroom
My story, will it be enough or back to the drawing board soon?
It's 12:30 AM and the kids are not home
Last minute changes nowhere to roam
The North Star shines tonight and Ron is pleased
The edition is ready but not done with ease

Jesus

What if Jesus believed in science?
And on charlatans there was no reliance
And peace was made through the truth and heart
Not just blind faith, making a better start

Why not rewrite the Bible to reflect a logical mind?
While at the same time remaining to be kind
Why can't we make new beginnings and say?
Things will turn out according to love's way

What if pseudoscience was gone and the mind enriched
What would happen if conspiracy theories were never pitched?
What if we chose to look at ourselves in the mirror?
Only to see there's nothing to fear

Love's pure light shines on the hill tonight
It reaches my heart and suggests a brand-new start
Embrace love and truth equally, that's what it's meant to be
A shining miracle that I can now more clearly see

Sands of Time

Time running out
Shout your last shout
Make it good this time
Make it scintillate and rhyme

Make it colorful and make it loud
Make it epic make it proud
Take it up top take it down low
Take it where you want it to go

The hourglass's clear warning
This is where our souls are soaring
Make it great make it your last stand
Standing proud, an honest and caring man

Science

Shocking how much medical science does not know
The best answers but so far to go
Science is the brilliant candle in the dark
Trying to prevent pseudoscience from making its mark

As I walk down the long dark tunnel of knowledge and reason
I know every paradigm shift will have its season
Please protect me from the cruel, brutal and wrong
As I attempt to sing my own courageous song

The light is sometimes dim but I walk toward the truth
Knowing the right path my conscience does soothe
Studying the reasons for us being here today
So logic and love can live, work and play

The Ocean

The tides rush in, the tides rush out
The ocean's beauty, we can't go without
The sea is the mystery all the wonder it has inside
The power and intensity she has nothing to hide

On her we sail
On powerful waves we prevail
The secrets of the deep
Are those that we keep
Captured by the ocean blue
Mother Nature giving us another clue

Hear the seagull's lonesome cry
On a peaceful island far and wide
Hear the sound of silence surrounding its shore
Calling us to come back for more and more and more

Last Christmas

Christmas time priceless beyond measure
Family togetherness, there's the treasure
Near the Christmas tree you and I and Mom and Dad
Thinking about limited time, leading to thoughts of happy/sad

Precious time, we share our souls
Living life the best, one of our top goals
Without caring we would surely die
Our rewards of love, we try and try and try

Survival of the fittest, but ruled by the laws of love
Finding a force which will help from above
This bond we create between family
Can cause us to pause and smile happily

Life

Life, full of opportunities and full of challenges
Problems exist but with joy's balances
Look for the victories ahead and the moments of meaning
Success possible whether left or right leaning

Can we gather the courage to live the ultimate life?
Or do we fall prey to discouragement and strife?
Is it possible to maintain a real winner's edge?
Before falling off the anguished ledge

Help us to live a life full of zest
And keep pride in everything we invest
Never give up the fight for the true and good
Love is around the corner in your neighborhood

Transition

Loved one when you transition to the other side
On your love, can I still confide?
You have broken through to the promised land
Where life and truth eternally stand

Trying to break away from my feelings tonight
As I hold your love tighter than tight
Your ghost is close I feel it near
As we on Earth continue to persevere

Oh love of mine -- separation is not kind
Because Earth and heaven cannot bind
But I feel you close in the summer breeze
And your love still sets my heart at ease

About the Author

Jeffrey McAndrew is the author of four published books. "My Heart At Ease" is his first published book of poems. His latest novel is called "Numinous" (published in 2019) and tells the story of a minister who questions his faith and his life. His first book "Our Brown-Eyed Boy"(published in 2003) concerns his family's struggles with his son Stephen's autism diagnosis. Jeffrey has worked nearly 20-years in the field of broadcast journalism at several radio stations in the Midwest and won numerous awards for writing and production. Some past accolades include: Fond du Lac Friend of Education Award in 1999, inducted into the Oshkosh North High School Hall of Fame in 2005, and Lakefly Writer's Contest 2nd place for his essay, "Three Questions for John Updike." (2017) Jeffrey is president of the Wordsmiths Writers Club in North Fond du Lac, Wisconsin and is also a member of the village's library board. He and his wife Debbie reside in North Fond du Lac.